The Story of America

Discover history with

American Girl

Consultant Glenda Gilmore, PhD

Contents

Introduction

Travel back in time with the BeForever™ characters. This exciting guide will show you what life was like for American girls in times past. You will be alongside your favorite characters for the key moments in the inspirational story of the United States and discover that girls have always shared hopes, challenges, and dreams—just like you.

When you see this symbol, always ask an adult to help you.

Changing fashions
Go on a journey through the history of American fashions—from mob caps to bell-bottom jeans.

Mob cap

Kaya™
1764

Felicity™
1774

Caroline™
1812

Josefina™
1824

Marie-Grace™ and Cécile™
1853

Kirsten™
1854

Everyday life

Find out what life was really like for girls in America's past—the homes they lived in, their daily chores, what school was like, and how they had fun.

> *Cécile Rey and Marie-Grace Gardner's (pp.22–25) Spanish-style courtyard, 1853*

Historic events

See the most important happenings in U.S. history through the eyes of the girls who lived through them.

> *Addy Walker (pp.30–33) prepares a feast to celebrate the end of slavery in 1865.*

Bell-bottom jeans

Addy™	Samantha™	Rebecca™	Kit™	Molly™	Maryellen™	Melody™	Julie™
1864	1904	1914	1934	1944	1954	1964	1974

Meet Kaya™

Kaya is a courageous Native American girl, growing up in the Nez Perce tribe before America became a country. The Nez Perce are hunter-gatherers, which means that during the warmer months, they travel through the forests and grassy plains of their Pacific Northwest homeland. They set up camp wherever they find a good source of food, and gather as much as they can to store for winter. Then, they move on when supplies run low.

Speak Nez Perce

Nez Perce (pronunciation)	English
tawts may-we (TAWTS MAY-wee)	Good morning
Eetsa (EET-sah)	Mother
Toe-ta (TOH-tuh)	Father

Clever crafts
The Nez Perce are famous for their beautiful basketwork and other crafts. When Kaya goes out to gather plants and herbs, she takes a useful patterned basket with her.

Baby dolls
Nez Perce mothers carry their babies on their backs in cradleboards just like the one Kaya uses for her doll. Mothers wear the cradleboards when they are on the move or doing chores.

Doll

Cradleboard

A helping paw

Tatlo the dog helps the tribe when it's time to move. His job is to pull bedding on a travois (sled) as the tribe moves camp.

Moccasins

Living off the land

Kaya and her tribe survive by gathering and hunting food. Everyone in the tribe is expected to do their part, so Kaya gathers plants, tasty roots, and berries in her basket.

Travois

America before the settlers

Long before European explorers arrive in North America, the land is home to Native American people, including the Nez Perce. Different tribes and cultures live all over North America. They live off the land by hunting, fishing, growing crops, or raising livestock.

Kaya's mare, Steps High

Rope bridle

Spotted markings

Fringed blanket under the saddle

Did you know?

In Kaya's time, the Nez Perce's homeland covered about 27,000 square miles of modern-day Idaho, Oregon, and Washingon.

★

The Nez Perce were given this name by the French. The tribe's name for themselves was Nimíipuu (nee-MEE-poo), which means "the People."

Riding the plains

With no paved roads, Kaya's people rely on horses to travel long distances. The Nez Perce, like many other tribes, train their own horses to help them travel and hunt.

1492 Voyage to America
Christopher Columbus sets out from Spain and lands in America. More explorers visit the "New World."

1500s New animals
Spanish explorers bring horses to North America. The animals allow Native Americans to travel faster.

On the move

There are no stores for Kaya's people to shop at. Instead, the tribe moves around to search for food. While they are on the move, the tribe sleeps in shelters called tepees, which are easy to transport, put up, and pack away. In the winter, Kaya's people move into permanent shelters.

Tepee

Fawn

Rabbit

Black bear cub

Mother nature

Kaya's people believe that the land does not belong to humans alone, but rather to all the creatures that live on it. It is every person's duty to respect nature, care for the animals, and share the land with them.

1621 First Thanksgiving
In Plymouth, Massachusetts, settlers from England share a meal with the Native Americans who have helped them learn to fish, hunt, and grow corn.

1770 Population grows
Two million settlers live in America. Philadelphia is the largest city.

Tea time

As part of her usual school lessons, Felicity learns to host tea time. She is taught the correct way to serve tea to her family and guests.

Tea set

Tea lesson gown

Fashionable furniture

Felicity's table and chairs have "Queen Anne" legs. The curved style is fashionable in the British colonies.

Queen Anne style legs

Meet Felicity Merriman™

Nine-year-old Felicity is growing up in Virginia—a colony, or settlement, that is ruled by Great Britain. Even though many colonists want to break away from Britain, Felicity and her family still follow many British traditions.

Popular pastime

Tea time reminds the colonists of their British background. Drinking tea is a part of everyday life in Britain and in the colonies.

Tea caddy

Creamer

Teapot

Serving tray

Cups and saucers

Sugar bowl

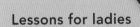

Lessons for ladies

Young ladies learn skills such as cooking, sewing, dancing, and playing musical instruments. Even though Felicity isn't old enough to play yet, she loves admiring the beautiful guitar that once belonged to her grandmother.

How to serve tea

✿ 🖐 First, warm a heatproof teapot. Ask an adult to help pour a little hot water into the pot, swirl it around, and pour it out.

✿ Add one teaspoon of tea leaves to the pot for each person, plus one more teaspoon of tea leaves.

✿ 🖐 Ask an adult to fill the teapot with boiling water. Leave to brew for four minutes exactly.

✿ Pour the tea through a strainer into a heatproof cup. Add a little milk or a slice of lemon and enjoy.

The American Revolution

Great Britain rules 13 colonies in North America. The colonists are angry that they must pay taxes to Britain and obey British laws that they have no say in creating. Many colonists want to break away and form a new country. The American Revolution begins when the colonists decide to fight Britain for their independence.

Did you know?

Many children in the 1770s played with wooden toys, including yo-yos, puzzles, and spinning tops.

★

The first American flag had 13 stars and 13 stripes—one for each colony.

Pinner cap

Choker necklace

Stomacher with pink ribbons

Colonial fashions

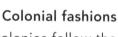

Ladies in the colonies follow the latest fashions from Europe. In 1774, the height of fashion is an open gown with a front panel, called a stomacher. Stomachers are interchangeable, so that ladies can update their look without having to sew a new gown.

1773 Boston Tea Party
As a protest against Great Britain making colonists pay high taxes to import tea, Patriots dump crates of British-owned tea into Boston Harbor.

1775 Fighting begins
Paul Revere and the Sons of Liberty spot the British army getting ready to attack. Fighting begins after he warns the Patriot leaders of the threat.

Patriots and Loyalists

The colonists who want to split from Britain, like Felicity, call themselves Patriots. Loyalists, including Felicity's friend Elizabeth, would rather stay under British rule.

Patriots and Loyalists have different opinions about who should rule the colonies. But many, like Felicity and Elizabeth, remain good friends.

Tricorn hat

Felicity is a Patriot

Elizabeth is a Loyalist

Military style

The tricorn, or three-cornered, hat, like Felicity's, is fashionable in the 18th century. Soldiers wear them on the battlefield during the Revolution. Military officers add embellishments, such as feathers, to show their higher ranks.

1776 Independence Day
On the 4th of July, the 13 colonies sign the Declaration of Independence. It states that the colonies are free from British rule.

1789 First President
George Washington becomes the first President of the United States of America.

A lakeside home

Caroline's formal parlor is full of nautical treasures, including a model ship. She can watch real ships sail on the lake from the parlor window.

Sailor's valentine

Sailor's souvenir

Caroline's favorite ornament is the sailor's valentine. The wooden frame holds a design made from the shells that a sailor collected on his voyages.

Meet Caroline Abbott™

Caroline loves living on the shores of Lake Ontario in New York. She especially likes sailing with her father, and dreams of being the captain of a ship one day. But Caroline's whole life is about to change when the U.S. goes to war with Great Britain in 1812.

Caroline's guide to sailing terms

❀ **Bow:** Front of the boat.

❀ **Port:** The left side of a vessel.

❀ **Saltie:** A Great Lakes term for a boat that also sails in the ocean.

❀ **Starboard:** The right side of a vessel.

❀ **Stern:** Back of the boat.

On the water
Caroline has fun sailing on Lake Ontario. From her small skiff, she can watch bigger ships carry goods and passengers between New York and Canada.

Winter wonderland
When the lake freezes, Caroline can't sail. Instead, she straps ice blades onto her boots, wraps up warmly, and glides gracefully over the frozen water.

The War of 1812

After the United States gains independence from Britain, the new nation grows quickly. This makes the British nervous—they do not want the U.S. to become more powerful than they are. Britain also doesn't want the U.S. to trade with France, Britain's enemy. The disagreement turns into a three-year war.

Did you know?

About 7.5 million people lived in the United States in 1812. The population had grown from around 2.5 million people in 1776.

★

Most girls growing up in the early 19th century were taught how to sew as part of their regular school lessons.

Sackets Harbor, New York

Caroline's peaceful hometown of Sackets Harbor on Lake Ontario becomes a U.S. Navy base during the war. The British navy set up their headquarters across the lake. Two battles take place in Sackets Harbor during the war.

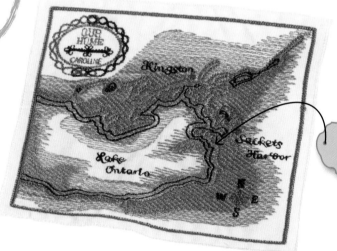

Sackets Harbor

1804–1806 Heading west

Lewis and Clark are the first to lead an expedition west of the Mississippi River. A Native American woman named Sacagawea is their guide for part of the journey.

1812 U.S. and Britain at war

The British refuse to let ships from other countries trade freely with the U.S., so the U.S. declares war.

Coping with hardship

During the war, many American families suffer great hardships when shipping and trading on the Great Lakes comes to a halt.

Families, like Caroline's, manage with what they can grow, buy, or raise.

Empire waist

Floral print design

Homemade fashions

The British block supplies from reaching small towns like Sackets Harbor. When people want to dress in the latest fashions, they make their own clothes out of what they have, just like Caroline does.

1814 White House fire The British set fire to many buildings in the nation's capital, including the Capitol Building and the White House (known as the Presidential Mansion). The U.S. and Britain make peace in 1815.

1821 High school for girls Teacher Emma Hart Willard opens a high school for girls in Troy, New York. It is the first high school to offer girls an equal education to boys.

Meet Josefina Montoya™

Josefina and her family live on a large farm called a rancho, near the city of Santa Fe in New Mexico. There's lots to do to keep a traditional New Mexican farm running smoothly! But Josefina loves to help her family by doing chores and learning to become a healer.

Herbs for healing
Josefina's aunt, Tía Magdalena, is a healer. She teaches Josefina to use herbs from her garden on the rancho as medicine.

Tía Magdalena's healing herbs

Yerba buena (YEHR-bah BWEH-nah): When anyone has a headache, Tía makes a healing tea from this minty herb.

Yerba mansa (YEHR-bah MAHN-sah): Tía chases away colds with this herb, which looks like spinach.

Handmade blankets
It takes a lot of people to keep the rancho running, and everyone in the family must help out. Josefina keeps the family warm at night by weaving warm, colorful blankets on a traditional loom.

Loom

Woven blanket

Yarn

Weaving fork

On the rancho

Josefina's rancho has been in her family for 100 years. She and her family grow crops and raise animals, including goats, mules, and sheep.

Helping out

During the harvest, Josefina joins her family to collect and store crops, such as corn and peppers. She helps her family bake bread and traditional meals in an outdoor oven for a harvest celebration.

Harvest outfit

Sombrita the goat

Trade routes

In 1821, New Mexico becomes part of Mexico, which declares independence from Spain. When a new trail from Missouri connects the U.S. to Mexico, American traders travel to Santa Fe for the first time. An exciting relationship develops between the two countries. In 1912, New Mexico joins the United States.

Trading ideas

New trade routes mean people in Mexico and the U.S. get to learn more about each other. When Americanos (American traders) come to Santa Fe, they get a glimpse of New Mexican life. Americans get to see New Mexican style, such as dresses, *rebozos* (shawls), and lacy fans—just like Josefina's—for the first time.

Fan

Rebozo

New Mexican style dress

Telescope from the U.S.

Traders' treasures

The city of Santa Fe, near Josefina's rancho, is at one end of a wagon trail that begins in Missouri in the United States. The trail is used by Americanos who bring new items, like this telescope, to Santa Fe.

1821 Mexican Independence
New Spain has fought for independence from Spanish rule since 1810. In 1821, New Spain gains its freedom. The nation is now called Mexico.

1837 College women
Oberlin College in Ohio allows female students to attend. Four women learn alongside male college students for the first time.

To market

Mexicans travel to the markets in Santa Fe to buy exotic American items. Some people travel great distances to exchange goods at the markets.

Market-goers need practial riding clothes and a hat to keep the sun away. Josefina's outfit is just right for going to the market.

Did you know?

Before Mexico gained independence, the land was called New Spain.

★

Other states were once part of Mexico, too, including Arizona, California, Colorado, Nevada, Utah, and Wyoming.

1848 Mexican-American War

After two years of war with Mexico, in 1848 the U.S. claims California, Nevada, much of Colorado, and almost all of Arizona and New Mexico.

1849 First woman doctor

Elizabeth Blackwell becomes the first woman to graduate from a U.S. medical school.

21

Meet Marie-Grace Gardner™ and Cécile Rey™

Nine-year-olds Marie-Grace and Cécile are growing up in New Orleans, Louisiana. The city is home to many French settlers. Like other girls their age, best friends Marie-Grace and Cécile enjoy European-inspired toys, games, books, and fashions.

Parlor fun
Cécile loves to play in her stylish parlor with her pet parrot, Cochon. Birds are popular pets in America, and Cécile gives her parrot a French name, just like her own.

Speak French with Cécile and Marie-Grace

Hello	Bonjour (bohn-zhoor)
How are you?	Comment vas-tu? (koh-mahn vah-tew?)
Very well, thank you.	Tres bien, merci. (treh byehn, mehr-see)
Good-bye	Au revoir (oh ruh-vwar)

Chemise (undergarment)

Crinoline hoop

French flair
Marie-Grace and Cécile wear stiff double hoop crinolines under their dresses. The hoops add fullness to the girls' skirts in the fashionable French style.

Sunday tradition

Marie-Grace and Cécile dress up in their Sunday best. Many people living in New Orleans keep the French custom of going for a walk on Sundays to spot the latest fashions and meet friends.

Puffed sleeves

Dainty white gloves

Lacy fan

Nation of newcomers

The Port of New Orleans in Louisiana is an important harbor that allows trade between the U.S. and Europe. Because of the port, New Orleans is home to many immigrants—people from different countries who move to the U.S. to settle. Many new cultures combine to make New Orleans a vibrant, exciting city in the 1850s.

Global mix

Many people move to New Orleans for business opportunities and to make a living. Settlers come from European countries, such as France, Ireland, Spain, and Germany, and other parts of the U.S., just like Marie-Grace.

Pitcher and bowl

Perfume bottles

Vanity stand

Face towel

Trade center

Residents of New Orleans, like Marie-Grace, can buy wonderful things that come all the way from Europe. Boats bring in goods, such as mirrors, toys, furniture, and fine fabrics.

1803 Louisiana Purchase
Congress buys a huge area of land called the Louisiana Territory from France. The U.S. doubles in size.

1838 Fast communication
Samuel Morse sends the first telegraph message in the U.S. Telegraphs transmit signals over a wire and allow people to communicate over long distances.

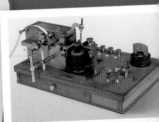

Did you know?

Many people enjoyed "parlor songs." The tunes were played on a piano and sung at home.

★

Children often went to fancy-dress balls, which meant they got to wear fanciful costumes.

Mardi Gras

Many people in New Orleans look forward to the French celebration of Mardi Gras, which marks the 40 days of fasting before Easter.

Cécile and Marie-Grace enjoy dancing, sweets, and dressing up in costumes when they attend balls.

Mardi Gras mask

Feather-like fan

1852 Woman abolitionist Harriet Beecher Stowe writes *Uncle Tom's Cabin* to show the hardships of life as a slave. It becomes popular around the world.

1853 Yellow fever An outbreak of yellow fever results in the death of more than 7,500 people in New Orleans.

Bright lights
The Saint Lucia wreath Kirsten wears symbolizes the coming of brighter days.

Swedish-style braid

Swedish holiday
Saint Lucia's Day is a holiday celebrated during the winter in Sweden to welcome the arrival of lighter days to come. Kirsten dresses up in a special outfit on this day.

Saint Lucia gown

Meet Kirsten Larson™

Kirsten and her family move from Sweden to America, and make a new life on the Minnesota prairie. But Kirsten's family doesn't want to leave their Swedish traditions behind. Even though they start new traditions in America they still enjoy Swedish holidays and customs.

Keepsakes

Kirsten brings special treasures with her to Minnesota. These items help her remember their home in Sweden.

Trunk for transporting and storing Kirsten's treasures

Necklace from Grandmother

Embroidered handkerchief

Sari, Kirsten's rag doll from Sweden

Traditional Swedish spoon bag

Warm winter clothes

Kirsten wears a hat, mittens, and sweater with a traditional Scandinavian pattern. They keep her warm during the winter and remind her of Sweden.

Start a new tradition

1. Think of something everyone in your family enjoys. For example, if everyone loves music, you could sing a special song together one day each year.

2. Pick a date. Maybe your new tradition will happen on a holiday, such as Thanksgiving.

3. Keep the tradition going every year. It will become a special moment for you and your family to share.

America's pioneers

1843–1858

Families like Kirsten's are called pioneers. Many of them are immigrants who move west to settle in the newer parts of America, called the frontiers. Most of the pioneers are farmers hoping to make a living from the land. Some of them travel thousands of miles, from their homes in Europe, to start a new life in the West.

Milk bucket

Work dress

School days

Children of all ages are taught together by one teacher in small, one-room schoolhouses. Paper is scarce, so students use chalk to do their schoolwork on pieces of slate.

Kirsten practices spelling on a piece of slate.

Dd dog

Hard work

Everyone in the family has chores. Children's jobs include looking after chickens, fetching water from the well, and milking cows. A bucket like Kirsten's is perfect for carrying fresh milk or water from the well.

1841 Oregon Trail
The first train of covered wagons carries 70 settlers 2,000 miles from Missouri to Oregon on the west coast. The journey takes about three months.

1848 Women's rights
Activists demand equal rights for women at Seneca Falls, New York. 300 women and men attend and pass 12 resolutions calling for equal rights for women.

Did you know?

The most popular way to travel from the east coast—where newcomers arrive—to the west was by train or boat and then covered wagons.

★

Children didn't go to school all year round. In the spring and fall, they stayed home to help plant and harvest the family's crops.

Cabins are small. There is not room for much furniture. Most furnishings, such as tables, chairs, and beds, are handmade out of wood.

Home sweet home

Pioneers must make or build almost everything they need. Each family's first task is to build a cabin to live in. These simple buildings are made out of logs cut from nearby forests.

1849 Gold rush
Settlers find gold in the rocks and streams of California. More than 100,000 people rush to San Francisco to search for gold.

1862 Homestead Act
A new law allows anyone to claim 160 acres of land if they build a house on it and live there for five years.

Time for school

In Philadelphia, Addy is thrilled to have the chance to go to school for the first time. In slavery, children received little or no education because it was illegal to teach slaves to read and write.

Fashionable trim

Lunch pail

New clothes

Addy's mother is a skilled seamstress. Momma made this new dress for Addy to wear to the spelling bee—and Addy won!

Meet Addy Walker™

Addy and her mother escape slavery in North Carolina to live in Philadelphia, Pennsylvania, where slavery is outlawed. Addy loves her new life, but she misses the rest of her family. Addy dreams of a time when they will all be free and can be together again.

Addy's top tips for school success

1. Do your homework every day. Learning is a gift.

2. Eat a healthy lunch. Momma includes "spelling" cookies to show Addy she loves her.

3. Ask for help. Addy and her friend Sarah help each other with difficult subjects.

Healthy lunch

Abacus, or number frame, for solving math problems

Slate chalkboard for practicing handwriting, addition, and subtraction

School desk and bench

Star student

Addy loves learning, and she hopes to become a teacher one day. She works extra hard at school to make up for the time she lost when she was enslaved. With her slate and chalk, schoolbook, and abacus, Addy will learn the three "Rs"—reading, writing, and arithmetic (math)—in no time.

1861–1865

The Civil War

Many plantations and large households in the south rely on enslaved people—unpaid workers with no rights who are owned by the planters and homeowners. By the 1850s, there is a growing movement against slavery, especially in the northern states. But the southern states want to break away from the United States and keep their slaves. In 1861, the bitter disagreement between the north and south turns into the Civil War.

A fresh start

Abolitionists, who want to end slavery, give escaping people help and new clothes for a fresh start in freedom. Addy gets a pink dress when she and Momma flee north, where slavery is illegal and they can be free.

Pincushion

Measuring tape

New clothes

Most slaves must leave everything they own behind when they escape to freedom. Because money is tight, many free people make their own clothes by hand, just like Addy's momma.

1860 Abraham Lincoln
Abraham Lincoln is elected President of the United States. He does not want slavery to expand into the west.

1861 Civil War begins
11 slave-owning states break away from the Union and form their own country, called the Confederate States of America.

Patriotic lantern

Did you know?

During the Civil War, many children played with toy soldiers. They made the toys out of wooden clothespins.

★

People escaping slavery sang songs to pass secret codes to each other. The messages included directions to the north.

The end of slavery

In 1863, President Lincoln issues the Emancipation Proclamation. It says that all slaves who escaped to the north are free. When the south surrenders in 1865, all enslaved people are freed.

Many freed people, like Addy, dress up in their best outfits and celebrate the end of slavery with parades and speeches.

1863 Harriet Tubman
Former slave Harriet Tubman makes return trips to the south. She leads hundreds of enslaved people to freedom in the Union Territory (north).

1865 Lincoln killed
A week after the Union wins the last major battle of the Civil War, Confederate sympathizer John Wilkes Booth assassinates President Lincoln.

Meet Samantha Parkington™

Samantha is growing up at the start of a new century, and the world is changing fast. Samantha is excited by new ideas, but her grandmother, Grandmary, insists that the old ways of doing things are best. Sometimes, Samantha feels torn between the two worlds she lives in.

Artistic ambitions

Painting and drawing are popular hobbies for young ladies at the turn of the century. Samantha's dream is to be a professional painter one day, like her hero, the famous American artist Mary Cassatt.

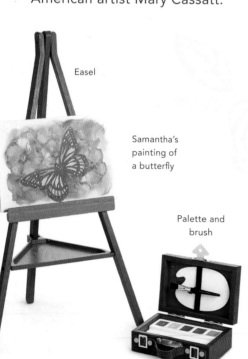

Two-wheeled travel

Bicycles are joining the horse and carriage as a fast way to get around town. Even though Grandmary does not like it, Samantha wears special cycling bloomers so that she can ride comfortably.

Easel

Samantha's painting of a butterfly

Palette and brush

Paint set

Make your own sketchbook

1. Stack 10 sheets of paper on top of each other. The sheets must be the same size.

2. ✋ Ask an adult to make two holes along one side of the stack of paper.

3. Thread a piece of colored ribbon through the holes and tie it in a bow.

Dressed up

Samantha's frilly dress and stylish coat are just what young ladies are expected to wear at the turn of the century. But Samantha finds it hard to act like a young lady all the time.

Spring coat

Lacy shade

Samantha's parasol shades her from the sun when she is outdoors. She doesn't want to get sunburned.

35

Turn of the century

At the start of a new century, the pace of change in the U.S. is bewilderingly fast. Exciting inventions are beginning to transform the way people live and work. But for now, the lives of most of the women and girls in Samantha's world are still focused on home and family life.

Samantha's friend Nellie

School dress

Schoolbook

Did you know?

Amelia Bloomer popularized bloomers (loose-fitting pants) for women. She believed that ladies should wear comfortable fashions for activities such as cycling.

★

There were many new inventions in the early 1900s, including the vacuum cleaner, the automobile, and the airplane.

School life

Wealthy students, like Samantha, learn subjects such as reading, penmanship (handwriting), needlework, and how to make polite conversation. Often, poor children, like Samantha's friend Nellie, must leave school in order to work and earn money to help support their families.

1879 New lights
Thomas Edison invents the electric light bulb. Electric lighting begins to replace candles, and gas and oil lamps.

1886 The Statue of Liberty
The people of France give this statue to the U.S. to celebrate Union victory in the Civil War. It is also a symbol of friendship between the two countries.

New treat

The invention of electricity and ice boxes mean that ice cream can be made quickly and kept cool in stores. Before now, ice cream was made by hand at home and had to be eaten before it melted.

People across America, including Samantha, love going to fancy ice cream parlors to enjoy delicious frozen treats.

Teddy bear

Presidential toy

During a hunting trip, President Theodore "Teddy" Roosevelt would not shoot a bear. A toymaker designed a stuffed bear and named it "Teddy's bear" after the President. Teddies, like Samantha's, become a popular toy.

1903 First flight Brothers Orville and Wilbur Wright become the first people to fly an airplane. They travel 852 feet in 59 seconds.

1908 Automobiles Inventor Henry Ford launches the Model T car. The cars are affordable for many Americans.

Happy Hanukkah

Rebecca and her family celebrate Hanukkah, the Jewish Festival of Lights. The traditional way to celebrate is by lighting candles and exchanging small gifts.

Shamash

Menorah

Hanukkah lights

On each day of the eight-day festival, Rebecca lights a new candle in the menorah. She uses a special candle called the *shamash* to light them.

Meet Rebecca Rubin™

Rebecca is a Jewish girl living in New York City with her parents, grandparents, and siblings. Rebecca honors the traditions of her faith and her Russian heritage, but she also has modern American dreams like becoming a movie star.

Special dinner

Every Friday evening, Rebecca and her family mark the start of the Sabbath, the traditional day of prayer and rest, with a special meal.

Traditional Russian urn called a samovar

Sabbath candles

Teapot

Scalloped cloth to cover the bread before it is blessed

Play the dreidel game

1. Any number of people can play. Everyone starts out with an equal stack of coins.

2. Each player puts a coin in the middle, and the first person spins the dreidel. Depending on the Hebrew letter it lands on, the player does one of these actions:
ג (gimel): takes all the coins from the middle
ה (hey): takes half the coins
ש (shin): puts in another coin
נ (nun): does nothing

3. Everyone takes a turn spinning the dreidel, until one person gets all the coins. That person is the winner!

Coins for the dreidel game

The dreidel has a different Hebrew letter on each of its four sides.

Russian heirloom

Rebecca treasures this necklace, which her grandmother brought to the United States when she moved from Russia, her home country. The necklace reminds Rebecca of her family history, which she is very proud of.

Newcomers

By 1914, New York City is the largest city in the U.S. People from other countries, called immigrants, settle in areas where people from the same places already live. Jewish people form the largest group of immigrants in New York and many, like Rebecca's family, live on the city's Lower East Side.

Music at home

Before the invention of the phonograph, the only way people could enjoy music at home was to make it themselves by playing musical instruments. The phonograph allows millions of people to enjoy listening to music on records in their homes.

American flag

School notebook and patriotic songbook

Phonograph

U.S. patriots

While they respect their families' customs and heritage, children of immigrants, like Rebecca, are also encouraged to be proud American citizens. At school, children learn patriotic songs and recite the "Pledge of Allegiance" every morning.

1880 Jewish settlers
Jewish immigrants begin to travel from eastern Europe to the U.S. About two million Jews arrive by 1914.

1914 Europe at War
World War I begins. The whole of Europe is at war when the U.S. joins in 1917. The war ends in 1918, but millions have lost their lives.

America is crazy about the movies in 1914. Just like Rebecca, many children enjoy dressing up as glamorous movie stars.

Newsreels

When World War I breaks out in Europe in 1914, movie newsreels help keep America's immigrants informed about what is happening in their home countries.

Did you know?

Jewish families moved from Russia to escape attacks, called pogroms, on their villages, and harsh laws that stopped Jews from earning a living.

★

One of the most popular records in 1914 was "Take Me Out to the Ballgame," a song about baseball.

1920 Women's rights
Women win the right to vote after fighting for it for 80 years.

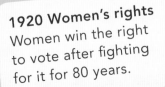

1927 At the movies
The Jazz Singer, the first full-length "talkie" (movie with sound), is released and is an instant smash hit.

Secondhand shirt

Homemade
Like most families in the 1930s, Kit's family doesn't have a lot of money. Most of her clothes are homemade with whatever fabric they can find—even chicken feed sacks!

Nose for news
Kit finds a basset hound with no owner. She decides to adopt the dog and name her Grace. Grace tags along with Kit when she's out looking for neighborhood news.

Kit's typewriter

Meet Kit Kittredge™

Nine-year-old Kit is growing up in the middle of the Great Depression in Cincinnati, Ohio, where she dreams of becoming a reporter. With some creativity, imagination, and plenty of can-do spirit, Kit has fun and brightens up the lives of her friends and family.

Ace reporter

Kit is tired of hearing sad news. She decides to write her own paper—the *Hard Times News*—which features happier stories right from her own neighborhood.

Hard Times News

Aunt Millie's Penny Pinching Poem

Use it up. Wear it out.
Make it do. Or do without.

Kit's Penny Pincher birthday party

Tools of the trade

Kit doesn't want to miss a big news story! She carries a pouch full of the tools she needs, including a notepad for recording the latest scoop and a pen for writing it all down.

Then she's off to type up the story on her typewriter—just like real reporters do.

Local newspaper

Camera case

Kit's news photos

Pouch for carrying supplies

Kit's Amelia Earhart doll

The Great Depression

In the late 1920s, the economy around the world slows down. Farm prices and wages fall, and banks close. The money that people put in the banks is lost. Many people lose their money, jobs, and homes during this time, known as the Great Depression.

Flying high

Record-setting flights are welcome good news. Some records are set by female pilots. Aviation dolls, like Kit's, become popular toys.

America's favorite game

Baseball games help Americans forget their troubles as they enjoy watching their favorite players take the field. Like Kit, many Americans also enjoy playing baseball to escape the hardships of everyday life.

1929 Stock market crash
The stock market crashes, and the Great Depression begins. Many people are unemployed or homeless.

1931 Dust Bowl
A severe drought destroys crops in the midwest. Nothing is grown there for almost 10 years. Many move away.

Grow your own food

Most Americans do not have enough money to buy groceries, so many people plant their own gardens. They also preserve their fruits and vegetables in jars. That way, they will have enough to eat during the winter months when it is too cold for fruits and vegetables to grow.

Many people take on lots of small jobs, such as laundry, to make ends meet. Everyone in the family helps out.

Preserving jar

1931 Tallest skyscraper
The Empire State Building in New York opens. It is 1,454 feet high and has 102 floors.

1937 Amelia Earhart
The female pilot becomes the first woman to attempt to fly around the world. Her plane is lost and she is never seen again.

Meet Molly McIntire™

Growing up on the American home front during World War II is not always easy for Molly. There are so many changes. Dad is away caring for wounded soldiers in the war and Mom is working at the Red Cross. Even everyday things, such as sugar, are in short supply. But Molly learns that she can make a difference during these uncertain times.

Helping out

The McIntires take in a guest. Emily comes all the way from London, England, where it is not safe for children to live during the war. Emily misses her family, but Molly helps her new friend feel at home.

Rationing

Since many things are rationed, Molly must learn to make do with what her family has. Many families, like Molly's, plant "Victory Gardens" and grow their own fruits and vegetables. This means that farmers can send more food to soldiers in the war.

Packed lunch

Molly packs vegetables from her Victory Garden in her lunchbox.

Plant a Victory Garden

1. ✋⭐ With an adult, decide where to plant your garden.

2. Buy some vegetable seeds and follow the instructions on the pack.

3. Water regularly and wait for your plants to grow.

4. Pick and eat your delicious victory vegetables.

Patriotic tiara

Miss Victory
This special dance costume is just for Molly. She gets to be Miss Victory and dance a solo in the spotlight.

Miss Victory costume

Hooray for the U.S.A.!
Molly can't wait to perform in the "Hooray for the U.S.A.!" show with her dance class. The show will raise money—and spirits— for the war effort.

World War II

1939–1945

In 1939, for the second time in the 20th century, the world goes to war. It starts when Germany, led by Adolf Hitler, invades other countries in Europe. The Allies, including Britain and France, join together to stop Hitler. Soon, the war spreads worldwide, with the U.S. joining in 1941. The war lasts for six years and more than 70 million lives are lost to the war.

British ration book

Less to go around

Molly's family has ration books like her British friend, Emily's. With foods, such as meat and sugar, in limited supply, each family is allowed only a certain amount. Molly needs stamps from her ration book to buy particular goods.

Over the airwaves

In 1944, people get their news and entertainment from the radio. There are all kinds of shows. American families also listen to regular war updates from President Roosevelt, which he calls "fireside chats."

Radio

1939 World War II begins
Germany invades Poland. The allied forces of Britain and France declare war. Italy and Japan join Germany's side.

1941 Pearl Harbor
Japanese bombers attack the U.S. Navy fleet at Pearl Harbor in Hawaii. The U.S. joins the Allies in the war.

Red Cross nurse doll

Snow globe

Women at war

Women are not allowed to fight during the war, but they have other important roles. Some become nurses to care for wounded soldiers. Others, like Molly's mom, help gather supplies for the Red Cross. Some women even work building planes and battleships.

Most soldiers who are fighting in the war send Christmas greetings home to their families. Molly gets the doll of her dreams from her father as a very special gift.

1945 War ends
The Axis powers (Germany, Italy, and Japan) surrender. The Allies (U.S., France, and Great Britain) win the war.

1945 United Nations
Representatives from 50 countries form the United Nations. The organization is dedicated to promoting international peace and security.

Birthday surprise
Maryellen usually wears hand-me-downs from her sisters. She is very excited when she gets this special new dress for her birthday.

Pink corsage decoration

Trendy puffy skirt

In the spotlight
Maryellen's new birthday dress is perfect for her variety show performance. She can finally bring her dream of being onstage to life—in style.

Meet Maryellen Larkin™

Maryellen Larkin has fun pretending to be a 1950s TV star and dressing up in Hollywood style. She has plenty of big ideas to help herself stand out from the crowd, but with five brothers and sisters, it's not so easy!

Hair curlers

Dress like a star

Give your hair the star treatment. Use rollers to create screen-ready curls.

★

Always dress your best. You never know when a Hollywood reporter might want to snap your photo!

★

Grab a pair of sunglasses. Stars always wear neat shades.

Baby-dolled up

Maryellen wants to be in style even when she drifts off to sleep. Her adorable baby-doll pajamas are right on trend.

Fashionable Mary Jane shoes

Cable-knit purse

Perfect accessories

Even when she gets stuck wearing clothes that have been passed down to her from her sisters, Maryellen still feels fashionable. She can dress up any outfit with the right accessories to make sure she fits in with the latest 1950s looks.

Lacy white gloves

Popular pearly bracelet and necklace

The 1950s

Americans are glad that World War II is over. Like Maryellen, they are full of hope for the future. Many people are better off than they have ever been. Jobs are easy to find and stores are full of new goods, including television sets and affordable, labor-saving home appliances, such as washing machines. These devices give people more free time.

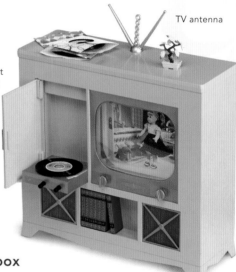

TV antenna

Television set with record player

Did you know?

TV shows were in black and white in the 1950s. Color TVs became popular in the mid-1960s.

★

The "space race" started when the U.S. and the Soviet Union (now Russia) competed to be the first to explore space. The Soviets won in 1957.

Magic box

Television quickly becomes the nation's favorite entertainment, even though there are only a few channels to choose from. The whole family gathers around the only TV set in their home to watch popular shows, including western dramas—Maryellen's favorite.

1956 Music star
Rock and roll singer Elvis Presley becomes a teen icon with the release of his record "Heartbreak Hotel."

1958 *Explorer I*
After a run of Soviet successes in the space race, the U.S. launches a satellite called *Explorer I*. It orbits the Earth.

Good times

In the 1950s, most people have money to spend—and free time to enjoy it. Going out to restaurants becomes a popular way to get together with family and friends.

The diner is a favorite place to meet. Customers enjoy hot dogs and milk shakes, and they play the latest rock and roll hits on the jukebox.

Jukebox

Two-tiered lamp shade

Poodle with cat-eye style glasses

TV Guide Magazine

Home comforts

Families, like Maryellen's, gather in the living room to relax, read, and watch TV. A stylish boomerang-shaped table is perfect for holding their newspapers and magazines.

1959 New states
Alaska and Hawaii become the 49th and 50th states of the U.S. They are the last two states to join the Union.

1960 JFK
John F. Kennedy (JFK) is elected as President. At 43, he is the youngest President to serve.

Meet Melody Ellison™

Nine-year-old Melody is growing up in Detroit, Michigan, during a time of change for African Americans. Melody and her family join the civil rights movement, a campaign for African Americans to have equal rights as white Americans. Whether it's speaking out for equal rights or singing, Melody uses her voice to make the world a better place for all.

Sing out!
Melody sings a solo for her church's Youth Day. Civil rights activist Dr. Martin Luther King, Jr.'s speech about equality inspires her to choose the perfect song. Melody raises her voice to stand up for what she believes in.

Popular songs from the 1960s

1. "I Heard It Through the Grapevine" by Marvin Gaye, 1968

2. "Baby Love" by The Supremes, 1964

3. "Fingertips (Part 2)" by Stevie Wonder, 1963

4. "I Can't Get Next to You" by The Temptations, 1969

5. "Please Mr. Postman" by the Marvelettes, 1961

Table and treats for a block party

Bingo cage

Bingo card

Make our Neighborhood Bloom!

Neighborhood block club sign

Community spirit
Melody loves helping her community as part of the neighborhood block club. Sometimes, the club gets together to have parties with food and games. Melody and her friends make plans to clean up a neighborhood park and make it safe to use again.

In the studio

Melody joins her brother Dwayne in a real music studio when he records a song for a big record label!

Recording tape

Control panel

10:00 Session Melody

Backup singer

Dwayne asks Melody to sing with him. Melody can't believe she gets to add her voice to a real record.

The civil rights movement

Even many years after slavery was made illegal in the U.S., African Americans do not have the same rights as white Americans. Many are treated badly at school and work. Some African Americans are not allowed to vote. The call for equality grows into the civil rights movement, a campaign that demands justice, change, and equal rights.

Ticket to freedom march

March for justice

Melody's home city of Detroit is a center of civil rights activism. At the Walk to Freedom event on June 23, 1963, 125,000 people gather in the city to support African Americans in the south and ease discrimination in the north.

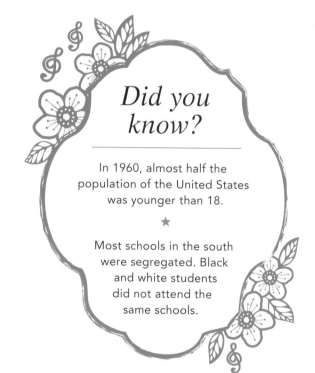

Did you know?

In 1960, almost half the population of the United States was younger than 18.

★

Most schools in the south were segregated. Black and white students did not attend the same schools.

1955 Rosa Parks
African American Rosa Parks is arrested when she refuses to obey segregation laws and give her seat on a bus to a white person. African Americans organize more protests.

1959 A new sound
African American songwriter Berry Gordy starts his own record label in Detroit. It becomes one of the most successful African American-owned businesses in the world.

Say it with a song

Some African American singers use music to be heard, just like Melody. Many new songs, such as Gladys Knight and the Pips' "Friendship Train," which calls for justice and equality, include messages that are key to the civil rights movement.

Every voice counts

Whether it's attending a march, standing up to injustice, or simply wearing a button to show support for equal rights, everyone can make a difference.

Civil rights button

1964 Civil Rights Act

A new law makes it illegal to discriminate against anyone based on their religion, race, or gender in places open to the public, such as schools, restaurants, and workplaces.

1969 Man on the moon

The U.S. Apollo 11 mission lands on the moon. Neil Armstrong becomes the first person to walk on the moon's surface.

Meet Julie Albright™

Everything is changing for Julie. After her parents get divorced, she has to move with her mom to a new neighborhood in San Francisco, California, and leave her old life behind. She learns that new ways of doing things can be exciting and fun, and she soon makes some changes of her own.

Change for good

Julie learns that bald eagles are endangered, and she wants to help save them. Julie organizes a car wash fundraiser with her friend Ivy. The money they make goes toward saving the eagles.

Patchwork bandanna

Convertible

Julie's best friend, Ivy Ling

Window squeegee

Fundraiser sign

CAR WASH

Help save endangered animals

Don't litter. Garbage can make animals sick.

★

Volunteer. Give your time and help to an organization that cares for animals.

★

Hold a fundraiser. Donate the money you make to a wildlife charity.

Hoop hopes

Julie wants to play on her school's basketball team, but girls aren't allowed. She gets support for her cause by asking people to sign a petition, which asks the school to let girls join the team.

1970s style sunglasses

Beach day
Julie is always active. When she's at the beach, she enjoys swimming in the Pacific Ocean.

On a roll
Julie loves skating along the ocean with her older sister, Tracy. The girls take in the sights and sounds of the beach as they roll by.

Stopper acts as a brake

America's 200th birthday

A lot has happened in the 200 years since the United States became an independent country, and the 1970s bring even more changes. Fashion, music, and technology continue to develop. Attitudes are changing, too, as new laws give women the right to be treated equally to men in education and at work.

Red, white, and blue streamers

Happy birthday, America!

In 1976, Americans celebrate the Bicentennial, marking 200 years since the signing of the Declaration of Independence. The declaration stated that America would no longer be ruled by Great Britain. Everyone gets into the spirit. Julie even decorates her bike.

Patriotic stars and stripes

1972 A new magazine
Ms. magazine is launched. It is the first magazine to be published exclusively by women for female readers.

1983 Sally Ride
Astronaut Sally Ride becomes the first American woman to travel to space.

Loose
T-shirt

Sandals

Bell-
bottom
pants

Feminist fashions

New styles of clothing for women and girls, including pants, loose shirts, sandals, and flowing dresses, become more casual and very popular. They are comfortable and easier to move around in than many old-fashioned clothes.

Disco
ball

Did you know?

Many schools didn't have sports teams for girls. That changed in the 1970s when a new law said that schools had to provide equal sports facilities for boys and girls.

★

Millions of Americans took part in anti-pollution protests during the first Earth Day celebrations in April 1970.

At the disco

The 1970s brings a new style of music called disco. Disco combines lots of different types of music into a new sound that's perfect for dancing. Many people, including Julie, hit the dance floor. A mirrored disco ball lights up the room while groovy disco songs play.

1997 WNBA
Women play professional basketball for the first time when the Women's National Basketball Association debuts.

2016 Woman candidate
Hillary Clinton becomes the first female Presidential nominee from a major political party.

Glossary

Abacus
A frame with rows of beads used for calculating simple math problems.

Abolitionist
A person who supported the movement to end slavery.

Bloomers
Loose pants worn by women, mainly for athletics, in the early 20th century.

Colony
An area that is controlled by another country, which is usually located far away.

Crinoline (KRIH-nuh-lihn)
A full, stiff petticoat worn under a dress.

Emancipation Proclamation
An order issued by President Abraham Lincoln on January 1, 1863, that declared that all enslaved people were free.

Endangered
When a species of animal is at risk of dying out.

Frontier
An area far from established towns and cities where few people live.

Immigrant
A person who moves to another country to live and work.

Jukebox
A machine that stores records and plays music when money is put in it.

Newsreel
A short film showing recent news that was played in movie theaters from 1911–1967.

Petition
A written request made to an authority by a group of people who wish to change something in the authority's power.

Phonograph
A type of music player invented in 1877. It records sound and plays music.

Pioneers
People who are among the first to move to and settle in a new country.

Rancho
A ranch or area of land where families would live, grow crops, and raise animals.

Ration
The permitted amount of an item, which is restricted due to limited supply.

Skiff
A small boat usually for only one person.

Slavery
When someone legally owns another person, controlling where they live and forcing them to work without pay.

Stock market
A system for buying and selling shares, or parts, of large companies.

Travois (tra-VWAH)
A wooden frame attached to an animal, such as a horse or dog, used for pulling heavy loads.

Yellow fever
A deadly disease that causes yellowing of the eyes and skin. It is easily spread from person to person by mosquitoes.

Index

Acknowledgments

 Penguin Random House

Senior Editor Tori Kosara
Designers Jenny Edwards and Jaynan Spengler
Additional Design Sam Bartlett and Mik Gates
Pre-Production Producer Marc Staples
Senior Producer Louise Daly
Managing Editor Paula Regan
Design Manager Jo Connor
Art Director Lisa Lanzarini
Publisher Julie Ferris
Publishing Director Simon Beecroft

Written by Tori Kosara and Rona Skene
Consultant Glenda Gilmore, PhD

First American Edition, 2017
Published in the United States by DK Publishing
345 Hudson Street, New York, NY 10014

Page design copyright © 2017 Dorling Kindersley Limited
DK, a division of Penguin Random House LLC
17 18 19 20 10 9 8 7 6 5 4 3 2 1
001–298004–Feb/17

A catalog record for this book
is available from the Library of Congress.

ISBN: 978-1-4654-5689-2

DK books are available at special discounts when
purchased in bulk for sales promotions, premium,
fund-raising, or educational use. For details, contact:
DK Publishing Special Markets, 345 Hudson Street,
New York, NY 10014
SpecialSales@dk.com
Printed and bound in China

www.americangirl.com
www.dk.com

A WORLD OF IDEAS:
SEE ALL THERE IS TO KNOW

DK would like to thank Alex Belmonte, Dave Conant,
Heather Gomez, Sara Hereley, Nancy Price, Isa Primavera,
Barbara Stretchberry, and Sally Wood at American Girl, and
Charnita Belcher and Ryan Ferguson at Mattel.

Thanks also to Esther Ripley and Eleanor Rose for
editorial assistance, Lisa Eyre for proofreading,
and Helen Peters for writing the index.

Photo credits

The Publisher would like to thank the following for their
kind permission to reproduce their photographs:
Key: b–bottom; c–center; l–left; r–right

Alamy Stock Photo:
13br D. Hurst (US Constitution and Feather Pen)

Images © Dorling Kindersley:
16bl Jon Spaull / Lewis and Clark Interpretive Center, North
Dakota (Lewis and Clark with Sacagawea); 24bc Tim Ridley
(telegraphic receiver); 28bl Bruce Forster / National Historic
Oregon Trail Interpretive Center (covered wagons);
36br Susannah Sayler © Rough Guides (Statue of Liberty);
45br Dave King (Empire State Building); 53br (map of Alaska
and Hawaii); 57br NASA / JPL (Apollo 11)

For further information see www.dkimages.com

All other images © American Girl

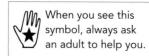
When you see this symbol, always ask an adult to help you.